THE MARKETING ANALYST'S HANDBOOK

DIPAMKUMAR RAVAL

Made with ❤ on the Notion Press Platform
www.notionpress.com

To all the aspiring and current marketing analysts who tirelessly turn data into actionable insights. Your dedication, curiosity, and passion drive business success and innovation. This book is dedicated to you and your relentless pursuit of excellence in the dynamic field of marketing analysis. May it guide you, inspire you, and equip you with the knowledge and skills needed to excel in your journey.

Contents

Foreword

In today's rapidly evolving business landscape, the role of a marketing analyst has become more critical than ever before. As companies strive to understand consumer behavior, optimize marketing strategies, and stay ahead of competitors, marketing analysts are at the forefront, turning vast amounts of data into actionable insights. The Marketing Analyst's Handbook is a comprehensive guide tailored for both aspiring and seasoned professionals in this dynamic field. It not only illuminates the core principles of marketing analysis but also equips readers with practical tools and strategies to navigate the complexities of modern marketing environments.

Preface

Welcome to The Marketing Analyst's Handbook, an indispensable resource designed to empower you with the skills and knowledge essential for success in marketing analysis. This book is structured to provide a thorough exploration of the key competencies required of a marketing analyst, ranging from foundational skills to advanced techniques. Each chapter is meticulously crafted to enhance your understanding of data interpretation, market research methodologies, and the strategic application of insights. Whether you're embarking on a career in marketing analysis or seeking to refine your expertise, this handbook will serve as your comprehensive guidebook and companion in unlocking the power of data-driven marketing strategies.

Acknowledgements

I would like to express my deepest gratitude to all those who have supported me throughout the writing of this book.

First and foremost, I want to thank my family for their unwavering love and support. Their encouragement and understanding have been invaluable to me during the writing process.

I would also like to thank my editor and publisher for their guidance and expertise. Their insights and feedback helped me to refine my ideas and present them in a clear and accessible way.

I am grateful to my colleagues and mentors, who have provided me with inspiration and guidance throughout my career. Their knowledge and wisdom have been instrumental in shaping my ideas about leadership and spirituality.

Finally, I want to thank my readers for their interest in this book. It is my hope that the ideas presented here will inspire and empower you to lead from within and enhance your spiritual quotient as a leader.

Thank you all for your support and encouragement.

Prologue

Introduction

In today's rapidly evolving business landscape, the role of a marketing analyst has become more critical than ever. As companies strive to understand consumer behavior, optimize marketing strategies, and stay ahead of competitors, marketing analysts are at the forefront, turning data into actionable insights. This e-book aims to provide a comprehensive guide for aspiring and current marketing analysts, covering essential skills, tools, and techniques needed to excel in this dynamic field.

Chapter 1: Understanding the Role of a Marketing Analyst

A marketing analyst is a professional responsible for interpreting market data to help organizations make informed decisions. This chapter explores the core responsibilities of a marketing analyst, including data collection, analysis, and reporting. It also delves into the importance of this role in shaping marketing strategies and driving business growth.

Chapter 2: Key Skills and Competencies

To be successful as a marketing analyst, one must possess a blend of technical and soft skills. This chapter highlights the essential competencies, such as statistical analysis, data visualization, critical thinking, and effective communication. It also offers tips on how to develop and enhance these skills through continuous learning and professional development.

Chapter 3: Data Collection and Analysis

Accurate data collection is the foundation of effective analysis. This chapter covers various methods of data collection, including surveys, interviews, and online tracking tools. It also provides insights into data cleaning, management, and analysis techniques, ensuring the data's integrity and reliability.

Chapter 4: Market Research Techniques

Market research is crucial for understanding market trends and consumer preferences. This chapter introduces different market research methods, such as primary and secondary research, qualitative and quantitative research, and the use of modern technologies like AI and machine learning in market analysis.

Chapter 5: Consumer Behavior Insights

Understanding consumer behavior is vital for creating effective marketing strategies. This chapter examines psychological, social, and cultural factors that influence consumer decisions. It also discusses how to analyze consumer data to uncover patterns and insights that can drive targeted marketing efforts.

Chapter 6: Competitive Analysis

Staying ahead of the competition requires a thorough understanding of the competitive landscape. This chapter outlines techniques for conducting competitive analysis, including SWOT analysis, benchmarking, and market positioning. It also provides strategies for leveraging this information to gain a competitive edge.

Chapter 7: Developing Marketing Strategies

A well-crafted marketing strategy is essential for achieving business objectives. This chapter explores the process of developing marketing strategies, from setting goals and identifying target audiences to selecting the right channels and tactics. It also emphasizes the importance of aligning marketing strategies with overall business goals.

Chapter 8: Measuring Campaign Effectiveness

Measuring the effectiveness of marketing campaigns is crucial for optimizing performance. This chapter discusses key performance indicators (KPIs) and metrics used to evaluate campaign success. It also provides guidelines on how to use data-driven insights to refine and improve marketing efforts continuously.

Chapter 9: Reporting and Presenting Findings

Clear and compelling reporting is essential for communicating insights to stakeholders. This chapter covers best practices for creating impactful reports and presentations, including data visualization techniques, storytelling, and tailoring content to different audiences.

Chapter 10: Trends and Future Directions

The marketing landscape is constantly evolving, with new trends and technologies emerging regularly. This chapter explores the latest trends in marketing analysis, such as big data, artificial intelligence, and personalization. It also offers predictions on future developments and their potential impact on the field.

Overview

The Marketing Analyst's Handbook provides a thorough exploration of the essential aspects of marketing analysis. From understanding the role and developing key skills to mastering data collection, market research, and competitive analysis, this e-book equips readers with the knowledge and tools needed to excel as marketing analysts. By embracing the insights and strategies presented, readers can enhance their analytical capabilities, drive business success, and stay ahead in the ever-changing marketing landscape.

ONE

UNDERSTANDING THE ROLE OF A MARKETING ANALYST

In the dynamic world of marketing, a marketing analyst plays a crucial role in steering organizations towards data-driven decisions. By meticulously interpreting market data, a marketing analyst helps businesses understand their target audience, optimize marketing strategies, and ultimately drive growth. This chapter provides a detailed overview of the core responsibilities of a marketing analyst and underscores the importance of their role in shaping successful marketing campaigns.

Core Responsibilities of a Marketing Analyst

1. Data Collection: At the heart of a marketing analyst's role is the collection of relevant data. This data can come from various sources, including customer surveys, social media analytics, sales records, and web traffic. The accuracy and comprehensiveness of this data are paramount, as it forms the foundation upon which all subsequent analysis is built.

2. Data Analysis: Once the data is collected, the next step is analysis. A marketing analyst employs various statistical tools and software to sift through the data, identifying trends, patterns, and correlations. This analysis helps in understanding consumer behavior, market trends, and the effectiveness of current marketing efforts.

3. Reporting: The insights gained from data analysis must be communicated effectively to stakeholders. Marketing analysts create detailed reports and visualizations that present complex data in a clear and concise manner. These reports often include charts, graphs, and dashboards that highlight key findings and actionable recommendations.

4. Market Research: In addition to analyzing internal data, marketing analysts conduct market research to understand external factors that influence business performance. This involves studying competitors, analyzing market trends, and gauging consumer sentiment. Market research helps businesses stay competitive and adapt to changing market conditions.

5. Strategic Planning: Marketing analysts contribute to the strategic planning process by providing data-driven insights that inform marketing strategies. They work closely with marketing teams to develop campaigns that are aligned with business goals and target the right audience. This strategic input is vital for crafting effective marketing messages and choosing the most impactful channels.

The Importance of a Marketing Analyst

The role of a marketing analyst is pivotal in today's data-centric business environment. Their work has a direct impact on the success of marketing strategies and overall business performance. Here are a few reasons why marketing analysts are indispensable:

1. Informed Decision-Making: By providing accurate and timely data, marketing analysts enable organizations to make informed decisions. Whether it's launching a new product, entering a new market, or adjusting a marketing campaign, data-driven insights ensure that decisions are based on evidence rather than intuition.

2. Enhanced Marketing Effectiveness: Marketing analysts help businesses understand what works and what doesn't. By analyzing the performance of past campaigns, they can identify successful tactics and areas for improvement. This continuous feedback loop leads to more effective and efficient marketing efforts.

3. Competitive Advantage: In a competitive market, having access to accurate market data is a significant advantage. Marketing analysts help businesses stay ahead of the competition by identifying emerging trends and opportunities. This proactive approach enables companies to innovate and adapt quickly.

4. Customer Understanding: A deep understanding of customer behavior is essential for creating personalized marketing experiences. Marketing analysts provide insights into customer preferences, buying habits, and pain points. This knowledge allows businesses to tailor their offerings and communication to meet customer needs more effectively.

5. Resource Optimization: Marketing budgets are often limited, and it's crucial to allocate resources wisely. Marketing analysts help optimize the allocation of marketing resources by identifying the most profitable channels and tactics. This ensures that every dollar spent on marketing delivers maximum return on investment.

In conclusion, the role of a marketing analyst is multifaceted and essential for driving business success in the modern marketplace. By collecting, analyzing, and interpreting data, marketing analysts provide the insights needed to make informed decisions, enhance marketing effectiveness, and maintain a competitive edge. Their work not only shapes marketing strategies but also contributes to the overall growth and sustainability of the organization.

TWO
Key Skills and Competencies

Success as a marketing analyst hinges on mastering a diverse set of skills. This chapter delves into the essential competencies required for the role, encompassing both technical abilities and soft skills. By honing these skills, marketing analysts can excel in their positions, driving meaningful insights and strategic decisions.

Essential Competencies

1. Statistical Analysis: A fundamental technical skill for marketing analysts is the ability to perform statistical analysis. This involves understanding various statistical methods, such as regression analysis, hypothesis testing, and correlation analysis. Proficiency in statistical software like SPSS, R, or Python is also crucial. These tools help analysts to draw accurate conclusions from data and identify significant patterns and trends.

2. Data Visualization: Presenting data in a visually appealing and easily digestible format is essential. Marketing analysts must be adept at creating charts, graphs, and dashboards using tools like Tableau, Power BI, or Excel. Effective data visualization helps in communicating complex insights to stakeholders clearly and concisely, facilitating better decision-making.

3. Critical Thinking: Critical thinking is a vital skill that enables marketing analysts to approach problems systematically and creatively. It involves evaluating information objectively, identifying biases, and considering multiple perspectives. Critical thinkers can make sound judgments and develop innovative solutions to complex marketing challenges.

4. Effective Communication: The ability to communicate findings effectively is paramount. Marketing analysts must be able to translate data-driven insights into actionable recommendations and convey these to non-technical stakeholders. This requires strong written and verbal communication skills, as well as the ability to create compelling reports and presentations.

5. Technical Proficiency: Beyond statistical tools and data visualization software, marketing analysts should be familiar with database management systems (e.g., SQL) and digital analytics platforms (e.g., Google Analytics). Technical proficiency ensures that analysts can efficiently extract, manipulate, and analyze data from various sources.

6. Market Research Skills: Understanding market research techniques is crucial for gathering valuable external data. This includes designing surveys, conducting interviews, and analyzing secondary data. Knowledge of both qualitative and quantitative research methods allows analysts to obtain comprehensive market insights.

7. Attention to Detail: Accuracy is critical in data analysis. Marketing analysts must have a keen eye for detail to ensure that data is correctly collected, analyzed, and reported. This minimizes errors and increases the reliability of the insights provided.

8. Adaptability: The marketing landscape is constantly evolving, with new tools, technologies, and trends emerging regularly. Successful marketing analysts must be adaptable, open to learning, and capable of quickly integrating new methods and technologies into their workflows.

Developing and Enhancing Skills

1. Continuous Learning: The field of marketing analysis is dynamic, necessitating a commitment to lifelong learning. Analysts should regularly attend workshops, webinars, and conferences to stay updated on the latest trends and technologies. Online courses and certifications in data analysis, market research, and related fields can also be highly beneficial.

2. Practical Experience: Hands-on experience is invaluable for developing technical skills. Working on real-world projects, whether through internships, freelance work, or collaborations, helps analysts apply theoretical knowledge to practical situations. This experience also enhances problem-solving abilities and builds a robust portfolio of work.

3. Networking and Mentorship: Building a professional network and seeking mentorship can provide guidance and support. Engaging with industry professionals through networking events, online forums, and professional associations offers opportunities for learning and career advancement. Mentors can provide personalized advice and share valuable insights from their own experiences.

4. Reading and Research: Staying informed about industry developments is crucial. Marketing analysts should regularly read industry publications, research papers, and case studies. Subscribing to newsletters, blogs, and podcasts focused on marketing analysis and data science can also help keep knowledge up to date.

5. Skill Development Tools: Utilizing online platforms and tools designed for skill development can be highly effective. Websites like Coursera, Udemy, and LinkedIn Learning offer courses on a wide range of topics relevant to marketing analysis. Participating in these courses helps analysts acquire new skills and enhance existing ones.

6. Collaboration and Teamwork: Working collaboratively with colleagues from different departments fosters a broader understanding of business operations. Marketing analysts should actively participate in cross-functional teams, sharing insights and learning from others. This collaborative approach can lead to more holistic and effective marketing strategies.

In conclusion, becoming a successful marketing analyst requires a diverse skill set that combines technical expertise with critical thinking and effective communication. By continuously developing and refining these skills, marketing analysts can provide valuable insights, drive strategic decisions, and contribute significantly to their organization's success.

THREE
DATA COLLECTION AND ANALYSIS

Accurate data collection is the foundation of effective analysis, forming the bedrock upon which marketing insights are built. This chapter explores various methods of data collection, including surveys, interviews, and online tracking tools. It also delves into data cleaning, management, and analysis techniques to ensure data integrity and reliability.

Methods of Data Collection

1. Surveys: Surveys are one of the most common methods for collecting primary data. They can be administered online, via email, or in person. Surveys allow for the collection of quantitative data on customer preferences, behaviors, and opinions. Designing effective surveys involves crafting clear, unbiased questions and ensuring a representative sample of respondents.

2. Interviews: Interviews provide in-depth qualitative data and insights that are not easily captured through surveys. They can be conducted one-on-one or in focus groups, either in person, over the phone, or via video conferencing. Interviews allow marketing analysts to explore complex topics, uncover motivations, and gain a deeper understanding of customer experiences and perceptions.

3. Online Tracking Tools: Digital analytics tools like Google Analytics, Adobe Analytics, and social media monitoring platforms are essential for collecting data on online behavior. These tools track website visits, page views, click-through rates, social media interactions, and other digital metrics. This data helps analysts understand user engagement and the effectiveness of digital marketing efforts.

4. Observational Studies: Observational studies involve watching and recording consumer behavior in natural settings. This method can provide valuable insights into how customers interact with products and services in real-world environments. Observational data is often used in conjunction with other methods to provide a comprehensive view of customer behavior.

5. Secondary Data Sources: Secondary data includes information collected by other organizations, such as industry reports, government statistics, and market research studies. This data can be a valuable supplement to primary data, offering broader context and helping to validate findings. Accessing and analyzing secondary data saves time and resources while providing valuable market insights.

Data Cleaning and Management

Once data is collected, it must be cleaned and managed to ensure its accuracy and usability. Data cleaning involves identifying and correcting errors, removing duplicates, and handling missing values. Effective data management practices help maintain data integrity and facilitate efficient analysis.

1. Data Cleaning Techniques:

- **Identifying and Correcting Errors:** Checking for inconsistencies and inaccuracies in the data, such as incorrect entries or outliers.
- **Removing Duplicates:** Ensuring that each data point is unique to avoid skewing analysis results.
- **Handling Missing Values:** Using techniques like imputation or data interpolation to address missing data points without compromising the dataset's integrity.

2. Data Management Practices:

- **Data Organization:** Structuring data logically, using clear labels and consistent formats to make it easy to navigate and analyze.
- **Data Storage:** Storing data securely, using cloud-based solutions or database management systems that ensure data is easily accessible and protected from loss or unauthorized access.
- **Data Documentation:** Maintaining detailed documentation of data sources, collection methods, and cleaning procedures to provide transparency and facilitate replication of analysis.

Data Analysis Techniques

With clean and well-managed data, the next step is analysis. Data analysis involves applying statistical methods and analytical tools to uncover patterns, trends, and insights that inform marketing decisions.

1. Descriptive Analysis: Descriptive analysis summarizes the main features of a dataset, providing a snapshot of the data through measures such as mean, median, mode, and standard deviation. Visualization tools like charts and graphs help in presenting descriptive statistics in an easily understandable format.

2. Exploratory Data Analysis (EDA): EDA involves examining datasets to discover relationships and identify patterns without prior hypotheses. Techniques such as scatter plots, histograms, and box plots are used to visualize data distributions and detect anomalies or outliers.

3. Inferential Analysis: Inferential analysis uses statistical methods to draw conclusions and make predictions based on sample data. Techniques like regression analysis, hypothesis testing, and ANOVA (Analysis of Variance) help in understanding relationships between variables and making generalizations about a population.

4. Predictive Analysis: Predictive analysis involves using historical data to make predictions about future events. Machine learning algorithms and statistical models, such as linear regression, decision trees, and neural networks, are commonly used for predictive analysis in marketing.

5. Prescriptive Analysis: Prescriptive analysis goes a step further by providing recommendations for actions based on data insights. It involves optimization techniques and simulation models to suggest the best course of action under different scenarios, helping marketers make informed decisions.

In conclusion, effective data collection and analysis are critical for marketing analysts to derive meaningful insights and drive strategic decisions. By employing various data collection methods, ensuring rigorous data cleaning and management, and applying robust analytical techniques, marketing analysts can uncover valuable patterns and trends that inform successful marketing strategies.

FOUR
MARKET RESEARCH TECHNIQUES

Market research is the backbone of understanding market trends, consumer preferences, and competitive landscapes. It equips businesses with the insights needed to make informed decisions and develop effective marketing strategies. This chapter introduces various market research methods, including primary and secondary research, qualitative and quantitative research, and the use of modern technologies like AI and machine learning in market analysis.

Primary and Secondary Research

1. Primary Research: Primary research involves collecting new, original data directly from sources. This method is tailored to specific research needs and provides up-to-date and relevant information.

- **Surveys:** Surveys gather quantitative data from a large audience. They are useful for understanding general trends and behaviors. Surveys can be conducted online, by phone, or in person.
- **Interviews:** Interviews provide qualitative insights through in-depth conversations. They help explore complex issues and gather detailed information on consumer opinions and experiences.

- **Focus Groups:** Focus groups involve guided discussions with a small group of participants. They provide qualitative data on consumer attitudes, perceptions, and reactions to products or concepts.
- **Observations:** Observational research involves watching consumers in natural settings to understand their behavior and interactions with products.

2. Secondary Research: Secondary research involves analyzing existing data that has already been collected by others. It is cost-effective and provides a broad understanding of the market.

- **Industry Reports:** These reports, often published by research firms, provide comprehensive data and analysis on market trends, competitors, and consumer behavior.
- **Government Publications:** Government agencies publish statistical data on demographics, economic indicators, and industry performance, which can be valuable for market analysis.
- **Academic Research:** Academic papers and studies offer insights into consumer behavior, market dynamics, and theoretical frameworks.
- **Online Databases:** Databases like Statista, Nielsen, and Euromonitor offer access to a wealth of market data and analytics.

Qualitative and Quantitative Research

1. Qualitative Research: Qualitative research focuses on understanding the underlying reasons, motivations, and opinions behind consumer behavior. It provides rich, detailed insights that help explain the "why" behind the data.

- **Methods:** Interviews, focus groups, and ethnographic studies are common qualitative research methods.

- **Benefits:** Provides deep insights into consumer attitudes and perceptions, uncovers hidden needs, and helps generate new ideas and hypotheses.

2. Quantitative Research: Quantitative research involves collecting numerical data that can be analyzed statistically. It is useful for identifying patterns, measuring variables, and making generalizations about a population.

- **Methods:** Surveys, experiments, and structured observations are common quantitative research methods.
- **Benefits:** Provides statistically reliable data, allows for hypothesis testing, and helps quantify market trends and relationships between variables.

Modern Technologies in Market Research

1. Artificial Intelligence (AI): AI technologies are revolutionizing market research by enabling faster, more accurate data analysis and providing deeper insights.

- **Text and Sentiment Analysis:** AI can analyze large volumes of text data from social media, reviews, and customer feedback to identify sentiment and key themes.
- **Predictive Analytics:** AI algorithms can predict future trends and consumer behavior based on historical data, helping businesses make proactive decisions.
- **Chatbots and Virtual Assistants:** These tools can conduct automated surveys and interviews, collecting real-time data from consumers.

2. Machine Learning: Machine learning algorithms can analyze complex datasets to identify patterns and relationships that traditional methods might miss.

- **Clustering and Segmentation:** Machine learning can group consumers into segments based on similar behaviors or characteristics, enabling targeted marketing strategies.
- **Personalization:** By analyzing individual consumer data, machine learning can create personalized marketing messages and product recommendations.

3. Big Data Analytics: The explosion of data from various digital sources has made big data analytics an essential tool in market research.

- **Data Integration:** Big data tools can integrate and analyze data from multiple sources, providing a comprehensive view of the market.
- **Real-Time Insights:** Big data analytics enables real-time monitoring of market trends and consumer behavior, allowing businesses to respond quickly to changes.

Combining Research Methods

Effective market research often involves combining multiple methods to gain a comprehensive understanding of the market.

- **Mixed-Methods Approach:** Combining qualitative and quantitative research provides both breadth and depth of insights. For example, qualitative interviews can explore consumer motivations, while quantitative surveys can measure the prevalence of those motivations across a larger population.
- **Triangulation:** Using multiple sources and methods to validate findings ensures the reliability and accuracy of the research. This approach helps cross-check data and identify any discrepancies.

In conclusion, mastering various market research techniques is essential for marketing analysts to gather accurate and relevant data. By leveraging primary and secondary research, qualitative and quantitative methods, and modern technologies like AI and machine learning, analysts can uncover valuable insights that drive strategic decisions and business success.

FIVE

CONSUMER BEHAVIOR INSIGHTS

Understanding consumer behavior is essential for developing effective marketing strategies. By examining the psychological, social, and cultural factors that influence consumer decisions, businesses can tailor their marketing efforts to meet the needs and preferences of their target audience. This chapter explores these factors in depth and discusses how to analyze consumer data to uncover patterns and insights that drive targeted marketing efforts.

Psychological Factors

1. Motivation: Consumer motivation is the driving force behind purchasing decisions. Understanding what motivates consumers—whether it's the need for security, social status, or self-fulfillment—helps marketers create compelling messages that resonate with their audience.

- **Maslow's Hierarchy of Needs:** This theory categorizes human needs into five levels: physiological, safety, social, esteem, and self-actualization. Marketers can use this framework to understand the underlying motivations of their target audience.

2. Perception: Perception is how consumers interpret information and form opinions about products and brands.

Marketers must ensure that their messaging is clear and aligns with the intended brand image.

- **Selective Perception:** Consumers filter information based on their beliefs and experiences. Marketers need to create messages that stand out and appeal to the target audience's perceptual filters.
- **Brand Perception:** The way consumers perceive a brand influences their purchasing decisions. Building a strong, positive brand image through consistent messaging and quality experiences is crucial.

3. Learning: Consumer behavior is influenced by past experiences and acquired knowledge. Marketers can leverage learning principles to shape consumer behavior.

- **Classical Conditioning:** Associating a brand with positive stimuli (e.g., pleasant music or attractive visuals) can create favorable attitudes toward the brand.
- **Operant Conditioning:** Rewarding desired behavior (e.g., loyalty programs) encourages repeat purchases and brand loyalty.

4. Attitudes and Beliefs: Consumers' attitudes and beliefs about products and brands significantly impact their buying decisions. Marketers need to understand and address these attitudes to effectively influence consumer behavior.

- **Cognitive Dissonance:** Consumers experience discomfort when their beliefs and actions are inconsistent. Marketers can reduce dissonance by providing reassurance and support after a purchase.

Social Factors

1. Family: Family influences play a significant role in shaping consumer behavior. Understanding family dynamics and decision-making processes can help marketers target their messages more effectively.

- **Family Roles**: Different family members may have distinct roles in the purchasing process. For example, parents may make decisions about household products, while children influence purchases of toys and entertainment.

2. Social Groups: Consumers are influenced by the groups they belong to, such as friends, colleagues, and social networks. Marketers can leverage these group influences to enhance their marketing strategies.

- **Reference Groups**: Consumers look to reference groups for guidance and approval. Marketers can use endorsements and testimonials from respected individuals or groups to build credibility.
- **Social Media**: Social media platforms amplify social influences, as consumers often rely on reviews and recommendations from their online networks.

3. Social Status: Social status and class can affect consumer preferences and purchasing behavior. Marketers need to consider the socioeconomic status of their target audience when crafting their messages.

- **Status Symbols**: Products that signify social status, such as luxury goods, appeal to consumers seeking to enhance their social standing.

Cultural Factors

1. Culture: Culture encompasses the shared values, beliefs, and practices of a group of people. Understanding cultural influences helps marketers tailor their messages to resonate with diverse audiences.

- **Cultural Norms:** Marketers must be aware of cultural norms and taboos to avoid offending their target audience and to align their messaging with cultural values.

2. Subcultures: Within larger cultures, subcultures exist with distinct values and behaviors. Marketers can target these subcultures with customized messages that address their specific needs and preferences.

- **Ethnic Subcultures:** Ethnic groups may have unique preferences and traditions that influence their purchasing behavior. Marketers can create culturally relevant campaigns to appeal to these groups.

3. Cross-Cultural Marketing: Globalization requires marketers to understand and adapt to different cultural contexts. Cross-cultural marketing involves tailoring strategies to suit the cultural nuances of various markets.

- **Localization:** Adapting products and marketing messages to fit local cultures and preferences is essential for success in international markets.

Analyzing Consumer Data

1. Data Collection: Collecting accurate and relevant consumer data is the first step in understanding consumer behavior. This can be done through surveys, interviews, online tracking, and social media monitoring.

2. Data Segmentation: Segmenting consumer data helps marketers identify distinct groups with similar behaviors and preferences. This allows for more targeted and effective marketing strategies.

- **Demographic Segmentation:** Grouping consumers based on demographic factors such as age, gender, income, and education.

- **Psychographic Segmentation:** Segmenting consumers based on their lifestyles, interests, and values.

3. Behavioral Analysis: Analyzing consumer behavior involves examining purchasing patterns, brand interactions, and product usage. This analysis provides insights into what drives consumer decisions and how to influence them.

- **Customer Journey Mapping:** Mapping out the steps consumers take from awareness to purchase helps identify touchpoints where marketers can effectively engage and influence them.

4. Predictive Analytics: Using predictive analytics, marketers can forecast future consumer behavior based on historical data. This enables proactive decision-making and the development of tailored marketing strategies.

- **Machine Learning Models:** Machine learning algorithms can analyze large datasets to identify patterns and predict consumer behavior with high accuracy.

In conclusion, understanding consumer behavior requires a comprehensive approach that considers psychological, social, and cultural factors. By analyzing consumer data and leveraging insights from various sources, marketers can develop targeted strategies that resonate with their audience, drive engagement, and ultimately lead to business success.

SIX

COMPETITIVE ANALYSIS

Staying ahead of the competition requires a thorough understanding of the competitive landscape. Conducting a comprehensive competitive analysis helps businesses identify their strengths, weaknesses, opportunities, and threats, enabling them to craft strategies that differentiate them in the market. This chapter outlines techniques for conducting competitive analysis, including SWOT analysis, benchmarking, and market positioning, and provides strategies for leveraging this information to gain a competitive edge.

Techniques for Conducting Competitive Analysis

1. SWOT Analysis: SWOT analysis is a strategic tool used to identify the internal and external factors that impact a business. It helps in understanding the strengths, weaknesses, opportunities, and threats related to competitors.

- **Strengths:** Identify the unique advantages and capabilities that competitors possess. This might include strong brand recognition, superior product quality, or efficient distribution networks.
- **Weaknesses:** Determine the areas where competitors are lacking or underperforming. These could be poor customer service,

limited product range, or outdated technology.

- **Opportunities:** Recognize market opportunities that competitors can exploit. This might include emerging market trends, technological advancements, or changes in consumer preferences.
- **Threats:** Identify external threats that could negatively impact competitors. These might include economic downturns, regulatory changes, or new entrants in the market.

2. Benchmarking: Benchmarking involves comparing a business's performance, processes, and practices with those of its competitors or industry leaders. This helps identify areas for improvement and best practices that can be adopted.

- **Performance Benchmarking:** Compare key performance indicators (KPIs) such as sales revenue, market share, and customer satisfaction levels.
- **Process Benchmarking:** Analyze specific processes and operations, such as supply chain management, marketing campaigns, and customer service practices.
- **Strategic Benchmarking:** Examine the strategic initiatives and business models of successful competitors to understand their approach to growth and innovation.

3. Market Positioning: Market positioning involves determining how a business or product is perceived in the minds of consumers relative to competitors. Understanding market positioning helps in identifying unique selling propositions and differentiating factors.

- **Perceptual Mapping:** Create perceptual maps to visualize how consumers perceive different brands or products based on various attributes, such as price, quality, and features.
- **Positioning Statements:** Develop clear positioning statements that articulate the unique value proposition and competitive advantage of a business or product.

- **Competitive Differentiation:** Identify and emphasize the distinct features or benefits that set a business apart from its competitors.

Leveraging Competitive Analysis for a Competitive Edge

1. Identifying Gaps and Opportunities: Competitive analysis helps identify gaps in the market that can be filled with new products or services. By understanding the unmet needs of consumers and the weaknesses of competitors, businesses can develop innovative solutions that address these gaps.

- **Product Development:** Create new products or enhance existing ones to meet the identified needs and preferences of the target audience.
- **Market Expansion:** Explore new market segments or geographic regions where competitors have a limited presence or where there is high demand for specific products or services.

2. Enhancing Marketing Strategies: Insights gained from competitive analysis can be used to refine and enhance marketing strategies. Understanding the strengths and weaknesses of competitors helps in crafting more compelling and targeted marketing messages.

- **Targeted Campaigns:** Develop marketing campaigns that highlight the unique features and benefits of a product, addressing the pain points and preferences of the target audience.
- **Competitive Messaging:** Use competitive messaging to directly compare products with competitors, emphasizing superior attributes and customer benefits.

3. Improving Operational Efficiency: Benchmarking against industry leaders helps identify best practices and operational efficiencies that can be adopted to improve overall performance.

- **Process Optimization:** Streamline processes and operations based on the successful practices of competitors, leading to cost savings and increased efficiency.
- **Technology Adoption:** Invest in new technologies and tools that competitors are using to enhance productivity, customer service, and innovation.

4. Strengthening Customer Relationships: Understanding competitors' customer service practices and customer satisfaction levels helps in identifying areas for improvement in customer relationships.

- **Customer Feedback:** Gather and analyze customer feedback to understand their experiences with competitors and identify areas where your business can provide superior service.
- **Loyalty Programs:** Develop loyalty programs and personalized marketing efforts that reward and retain customers, differentiating your business from competitors.

5. Anticipating Competitive Moves: Regularly monitoring competitors' activities and market trends helps in anticipating their next moves and preparing proactive strategies.

- **Market Intelligence:** Stay informed about competitors' product launches, marketing campaigns, and strategic initiatives through market intelligence and competitor monitoring tools.
- **Proactive Planning:** Develop contingency plans and strategic initiatives that can be quickly implemented in response to competitive threats or opportunities.

Implementing Competitive Analysis in Business Strategy

1. Continuous Monitoring: Competitive analysis should be an ongoing process rather than a one-time activity. Regularly updating competitive insights ensures that businesses stay informed about market changes and emerging trends.

- **Regular Updates:** Schedule periodic reviews of competitive analysis to incorporate new data, insights, and market developments.
- **Cross-Functional Collaboration:** Involve different departments, such as marketing, sales, and product development, in the competitive analysis process to gather diverse perspectives and insights.

2. Actionable Insights: Ensure that the findings from competitive analysis are translated into actionable insights and strategies that can be implemented across the organization.

- **Strategic Planning:** Incorporate competitive analysis insights into the strategic planning process, aligning business goals and initiatives with market opportunities and competitive advantages.
- **Performance Measurement:** Track the impact of competitive strategies on key performance indicators, adjusting approaches as needed to achieve desired outcomes.

In conclusion, conducting thorough competitive analysis is crucial for understanding the competitive landscape and identifying opportunities for differentiation and growth. By leveraging techniques such as SWOT analysis, benchmarking, and market positioning, businesses can gain valuable insights that inform strategic decisions and drive a sustainable competitive advantage.

SEVEN

DEVELOPING MARKETING STRATEGIES

A well-crafted marketing strategy is essential for achieving business objectives and sustaining growth. This chapter explores the process of developing effective marketing strategies, from setting goals and identifying target audiences to selecting the right channels and tactics. It also emphasizes the importance of aligning marketing strategies with overall business goals.

Setting Marketing Goals

The first step in developing a marketing strategy is to set clear, measurable goals that align with the overall business objectives. These goals should be specific, attainable, and time-bound to ensure they provide a clear direction for marketing efforts.

1. Define Business Objectives: Understand the broader business objectives to ensure that marketing goals support these targets. Common business objectives include increasing sales, expanding market share, enhancing brand awareness, and improving customer retention.

2. Set SMART Goals: SMART goals are Specific, Measurable, Achievable, Relevant, and Time-bound. These criteria help ensure that marketing goals are clear and attainable.

- **Specific:** Define the exact outcome desired (e.g., increase website traffic by 20%).
- **Measurable:** Identify how progress will be measured (e.g., using Google Analytics to track website traffic).
- **Achievable:** Ensure the goal is realistic given the resources and constraints.
- **Relevant:** Align the goal with broader business objectives.
- **Time-bound:** Set a deadline for achieving the goal.

Identifying Target Audiences

Understanding the target audience is crucial for developing marketing strategies that resonate and drive engagement. Identifying and segmenting the audience helps tailor marketing messages and choose appropriate channels.

1. Audience Research: Conduct thorough research to understand the demographics, psychographics, and behaviors of the target audience. Use tools such as surveys, interviews, and market research reports.

2. Segmentation: Divide the broader target audience into smaller, more manageable segments based on shared characteristics.

- **Demographic Segmentation:** Group consumers by age, gender, income, education, etc.
- **Psychographic Segmentation:** Segment based on lifestyle, values, interests, and attitudes.
- **Behavioral Segmentation:** Categorize consumers based on their behavior, such as purchasing habits, brand loyalty, and product usage.

3. Buyer Personas: Create detailed buyer personas representing different segments of the target audience. These personas should include demographic details, motivations, pain points, and purchasing behavior to guide marketing efforts.

Selecting Marketing Channels

Choosing the right marketing channels is critical for reaching the target audience effectively. A multi-channel approach often yields the best results, as it allows for reaching consumers across different touchpoints.

1. Digital Marketing Channels: Digital channels offer wide reach and precise targeting options. Key digital channels include:

- **Social Media:** Platforms like Facebook, Instagram, LinkedIn, and Twitter are powerful for brand awareness and engagement.
- **Search Engine Marketing (SEM):** Use paid search ads and search engine optimization (SEO) to drive traffic to your website.
- **Content Marketing:** Create and distribute valuable content to attract and engage the target audience. This includes blog posts, videos, infographics, and eBooks.
- **Email Marketing:** Use email campaigns to nurture leads, promote products, and maintain customer relationships.
- **Influencer Marketing:** Partner with influencers to leverage their audience and credibility.

2. Traditional Marketing Channels: Traditional channels still play a crucial role, especially for reaching specific demographics.

- **Print Advertising:** Newspapers, magazines, and direct mail.
- **Broadcast Advertising:** Television and radio commercials.
- **Outdoor Advertising:** Billboards, transit ads, and posters.
- **Events and Sponsorships:** Trade shows, conferences, and sponsorship of events.

3. Integrated Marketing: An integrated marketing approach ensures consistent messaging across all channels. Coordinate digital and traditional marketing efforts to create a seamless experience for the target audience.

Developing Marketing Tactics

Once the channels are selected, the next step is to develop specific tactics that will be used to achieve the marketing goals.

1. Content Creation: Develop high-quality content tailored to the interests and needs of the target audience. This includes blog posts, social media updates, videos, infographics, and more.

2. Campaign Planning: Plan and execute marketing campaigns that align with the marketing goals. Define the campaign objectives, target audience, key messages, budget, and timeline.

3. Personalization: Use data and insights to personalize marketing messages and offers. Personalized marketing improves engagement and conversion rates by making consumers feel valued and understood.

4. Automation: Leverage marketing automation tools to streamline and optimize marketing efforts. Automation can be used for email campaigns, social media scheduling, lead nurturing, and customer segmentation.

5. Analytics and Optimization: Regularly measure and analyze the performance of marketing activities. Use key performance indicators (KPIs) such as website traffic, conversion rates, engagement metrics, and return on investment (ROI) to assess success and identify areas for improvement.

Aligning Marketing Strategies with Business Goals

To ensure that marketing efforts drive business success, it is crucial to align marketing strategies with the overall business goals.

1. Strategic Alignment: Ensure that marketing goals and strategies support the broader business objectives. This alignment ensures that marketing efforts contribute to overall business growth and profitability.

2. Cross-Functional Collaboration: Collaborate with other departments, such as sales, product development, and customer service, to ensure a cohesive approach. Cross-functional collaboration helps align messaging, improve customer experiences, and achieve shared goals.

3. Regular Review and Adjustment: Regularly review marketing performance and make adjustments as needed. The business environment and consumer preferences change over time, so it is important to stay agile and adapt strategies accordingly.

In conclusion, developing a well-crafted marketing strategy involves setting clear goals, identifying target audiences, selecting the right channels, and implementing effective tactics. By aligning marketing strategies with overall business goals and continuously optimizing efforts, businesses can achieve sustained growth and success in a competitive marketplace.

TEN
TRENDS AND FUTURE DIRECTIONS

The marketing landscape is constantly evolving, driven by advancements in technology and changing consumer behaviors. Staying ahead of these trends is crucial for marketing analysts who aim to maintain a competitive edge. This chapter explores the latest trends in marketing analysis, such as big data, artificial intelligence (AI), and personalization, and offers predictions on future developments and their potential impact on the field.

Big Data

Big data refers to the vast volumes of data generated by digital interactions, including social media activity, online transactions, and sensor data from connected devices. This wealth of information presents both challenges and opportunities for marketing analysts.

1. Volume, Velocity, and Variety:

- **Volume:** The sheer amount of data available can be overwhelming. Advanced storage and processing solutions are necessary to handle this data effectively.
- **Velocity:** The speed at which data is generated and needs to be processed requires real-time or near-real-time analytics.
- **Variety:** Data comes in various formats, including structured, semi-structured, and unstructured data, necessitating flexible

EIGHT

MEASURING CAMPAIGN EFFECTIVENESS

Measuring the effectiveness of marketing campaigns is crucial for optimizing performance and ensuring a positive return on investment (ROI). By evaluating key performance indicators (KPIs) and metrics, marketers can gain valuable insights into what works and what doesn't, allowing them to refine and improve their efforts continuously. This chapter discusses the essential KPIs and metrics used to evaluate campaign success and provides guidelines on using data-driven insights to enhance marketing strategies.

Key Performance Indicators (KPIs) and Metrics

Selecting the right KPIs and metrics is essential for accurately assessing the performance of marketing campaigns. These indicators vary depending on the campaign goals, channels used, and target audience. Below are some common KPIs and metrics categorized by their relevance to different aspects of marketing.

1. Website Performance:

- **Traffic:** Measure the number of visitors to the website. Tools like Google Analytics can track overall traffic, unique visitors, and page views.

- **Bounce Rate:** The percentage of visitors who leave the site after viewing only one page. A high bounce rate may indicate that the content is not engaging or relevant.
- **Session Duration:** The average time visitors spend on the website. Longer session durations typically indicate higher engagement.
- **Conversion Rate:** The percentage of visitors who complete a desired action, such as making a purchase, signing up for a newsletter, or filling out a form.

2. Social Media Engagement:

- **Likes, Shares, and Comments:** Engagement metrics that indicate how users interact with social media posts.
- **Follower Growth:** The increase in the number of followers or fans over time.
- **Reach and Impressions:** Reach measures the number of unique users who see a post, while impressions count the total number of times a post is viewed.
- **Engagement Rate:** The percentage of followers who engage with the content, calculated by dividing the total engagement by the number of followers and multiplying by 100.

3. Email Marketing:

- **Open Rate:** The percentage of recipients who open an email. A low open rate may suggest issues with the subject line or sender reputation.
- **Click-Through Rate (CTR):** The percentage of recipients who click on a link within the email. A higher CTR indicates effective content and call-to-actions.
- **Unsubscribe Rate:** The percentage of recipients who opt-out of the email list. Monitoring this rate helps identify potential issues with email content or frequency.

- **Conversion Rate:** The percentage of email recipients who complete the desired action after clicking through.

4. Advertising Performance:

- **Click-Through Rate (CTR):** The ratio of clicks to impressions for online ads. A higher CTR indicates that the ad is compelling and relevant to the audience.
- **Cost Per Click (CPC):** The average cost of each click on an ad. Lower CPCs are desirable as they indicate cost-effective advertising.
- **Cost Per Acquisition (CPA):** The average cost to acquire a customer or lead through the campaign. Lower CPAs indicate more efficient marketing.
- **Return on Ad Spend (ROAS):** The revenue generated from an ad campaign divided by the cost of the campaign. A higher ROAS signifies a more profitable campaign.

5. Customer Metrics:

- **Customer Lifetime Value (CLV):** The total revenue a business can expect from a customer over the duration of their relationship.
- **Customer Acquisition Cost (CAC):** The total cost of acquiring a new customer. Lower CACs are preferable as they indicate more efficient marketing.
- **Net Promoter Score (NPS):** A measure of customer loyalty and satisfaction, typically obtained through surveys asking how likely customers are to recommend the business to others.

Using Data-Driven Insights

To refine and improve marketing efforts continuously, it is essential to leverage data-driven insights. Here are guidelines on how to effectively use these insights:

1. Regular Monitoring and Reporting:

- **Dashboard Creation**: Develop dashboards using tools like Google Analytics, HubSpot, or Tableau to monitor KPIs and metrics in real-time. This allows for quick identification of trends and issues.
- **Scheduled Reporting**: Generate regular reports (e.g., weekly, monthly) to track campaign performance over time. Compare these reports to historical data to identify patterns and areas for improvement.

2. Analyzing and Interpreting Data:

- **Trend Analysis**: Identify trends in the data to understand what is driving performance. Look for correlations between different metrics to uncover insights (e.g., increased social media engagement leading to higher website traffic).
- **Segmentation**: Analyze data by different segments, such as demographics, geographic locations, or customer behavior, to gain a deeper understanding of target audiences.

3. A/B Testing and Experimentation:

- **A/B Testing**: Conduct A/B tests to compare the performance of different versions of marketing assets (e.g., email subject lines, ad creatives, landing pages). Use the results to determine which version performs better.
- **Continuous Experimentation**: Regularly test new strategies, tactics, and channels to discover new opportunities for improvement. Document the results and learnings from each experiment.

4. Optimizing Campaigns:

- **Adjusting Strategies**: Use insights from data analysis to adjust and optimize marketing strategies. For example, if a particular ad channel is underperforming, reallocate the budget to more effective channels.

- **Refining Targeting:** Use data to refine audience targeting and ensure that marketing messages reach the most relevant and high-potential customers.

5. Enhancing Customer Experience:

- **Personalization:** Use data insights to personalize marketing messages and offers based on customer behavior and preferences. Personalized marketing enhances customer engagement and loyalty.
- **Feedback Loops:** Collect and analyze customer feedback to identify pain points and areas for improvement. Use this feedback to enhance the overall customer experience.

6. Leveraging Advanced Analytics:

- **Predictive Analytics:** Use predictive analytics to forecast future trends and customer behavior based on historical data. This allows for proactive decision-making and better resource allocation.
- **Machine Learning:** Implement machine learning models to analyze complex datasets and uncover deeper insights that may not be apparent through traditional analysis methods.

In conclusion, measuring the effectiveness of marketing campaigns through KPIs and metrics is essential for optimizing performance and achieving business objectives. By regularly monitoring, analyzing, and interpreting data, marketers can make informed decisions, refine strategies, and continuously improve their efforts. Leveraging data-driven insights not only enhances marketing effectiveness but also drives overall business success.

NINE

Reporting and Presenting Findings

Clear and compelling reporting is essential for communicating insights to stakeholders effectively. An impactful report or presentation not only conveys data but also tells a story that resonates with the audience. This chapter covers best practices for creating impactful reports and presentations, including data visualization techniques, storytelling, and tailoring content to different audiences.

Best Practices for Creating Impactful Reports

Creating effective reports requires careful consideration of the audience, the key messages, and the presentation of data. Here are some best practices:

1. Know Your Audience: Understanding the needs and preferences of your audience is crucial. Different stakeholders may have varying levels of familiarity with the data and differing interests.

- **Executives:** Focus on high-level insights, strategic implications, and actionable recommendations. Use concise language and highlight key takeaways.

- **Analysts and Technical Teams:** Provide detailed data, methodologies, and in-depth analysis. Include technical terms and data tables as needed.
- **Marketing and Sales Teams:** Emphasize insights that impact customer behavior, campaign performance, and sales strategies. Use visual aids and practical examples.

2. Define Key Messages: Identify the main points you want to convey in your report. Ensure these messages are clear and supported by the data.

- **Insights:** Highlight the most important findings from the data analysis.
- **Implications:** Explain what these findings mean for the business or project.
- **Recommendations:** Provide actionable steps based on the insights.

3. Structure the Report: A well-structured report is easier to follow and more effective in communicating the message.

- **Executive Summary:** Provide a brief overview of the key findings, implications, and recommendations.
- **Introduction:** Introduce the purpose of the report and the methodologies used.
- **Data Analysis:** Present the detailed analysis and findings, supported by data visualizations and explanations.
- **Conclusions:** Summarize the key insights and their implications.
- **Recommendations:** Offer clear and actionable recommendations based on the analysis.
- **Appendices:** Include additional data, charts, or technical details for reference.

Data Visualization Techniques

Data visualization is a powerful tool for making data more understandable and impactful. Here are some techniques to enhance your reports and presentations:

1. Choose the Right Chart Type: Select the chart type that best represents the data and makes it easy to interpret.

- **Bar Charts:** Ideal for comparing quantities across categories.
- **Line Charts:** Useful for showing trends over time.
- **Pie Charts:** Effective for illustrating proportions and percentages.
- **Scatter Plots:** Great for showing relationships between two variables.
- **Heat Maps:** Useful for displaying data density and highlighting patterns.

2. Keep It Simple: Avoid clutter and focus on clarity. Use clean, simple designs that highlight the key data points.

- **Limit Colors:** Use a consistent color scheme and avoid using too many colors.
- **Use Labels:** Clearly label axes, data points, and legends to ensure the chart is easy to understand.
- **Highlight Key Data:** Use contrasting colors or bold fonts to draw attention to important data points.

3. Tell a Story with Data: Use data visualizations to support the narrative and guide the audience through the insights.

- **Contextualize Data:** Provide context for the data by including benchmarks, targets, or historical trends.
- **Sequence Visuals:** Arrange charts and graphs in a logical sequence that builds the narrative.
- **Annotations:** Use annotations to explain key insights directly on the chart.

Storytelling in Reports and Presentations

Storytelling is a powerful way to make data more engaging and memorable. Here are some tips for incorporating storytelling into your reports and presentations:

1. Create a Narrative Arc: Structure your report or presentation with a clear beginning, middle, and end.

- **Introduction:** Set the stage by explaining the purpose and importance of the analysis.
- **Development:** Present the data and insights, building the story with logical progression.
- **Conclusion:** Summarize the findings and emphasize the key takeaways.

2. Use Real-World Examples: Illustrate your points with real-world examples or case studies that relate to the audience's experience.

- **Customer Stories:** Share stories of how customers have benefited from a product or service.
- **Market Trends:** Provide examples of market trends that are relevant to the audience's industry.

3. Engage Emotions: Connect with the audience on an emotional level to make the story more compelling.

- **Visual Imagery:** Use visuals that evoke emotions and reinforce the message.
- **Personal Anecdotes:** Share personal experiences or anecdotes that relate to the data.

Tailoring Content to Different Audiences

Different audiences have different needs and preferences. Tailoring your content ensures that the message is relevant and impactful.

1. Executive Audience: Focus on strategic insights and high-level recommendations.

- **Brevity:** Keep the presentation concise and to the point.
- **Visuals:** Use simple, high-impact visuals to illustrate key points.
- **Actionable Insights:** Emphasize actionable insights and strategic implications.

2. Technical Audience: Provide detailed data, methodologies, and technical explanations.

- **Depth:** Include detailed analysis and technical details.
- **Clarity:** Ensure that technical terms and methodologies are clearly explained.
- **Accuracy:** Provide accurate and precise data to support the findings.

3. General Audience: Simplify the content and focus on practical implications.

- **Clarity:** Avoid jargon and technical terms. Use simple language.
- **Engagement:** Use engaging visuals and storytelling techniques.
- **Relevance:** Emphasize the practical implications and benefits of the findings.

Presenting Findings

Presenting findings effectively requires good preparation and delivery. Here are some tips:

1. Preparation:

- **Rehearse:** Practice the presentation multiple times to ensure smooth delivery.
- **Anticipate Questions:** Prepare for potential questions and have answers ready.

- **Technical Setup:** Ensure all technical equipment (projector, microphone, etc.) is set up and tested.

2. Delivery:

- **Confidence:** Present with confidence and enthusiasm.
- **Clarity:** Speak clearly and at a moderate pace. Avoid jargon and technical terms.
- **Engagement:** Maintain eye contact with the audience and encourage interaction.

3. Follow-Up:

- **Q&A Session:** Allow time for questions and provide clear, concise answers.
- **Feedback:** Collect feedback from the audience to improve future presentations.
- **Action Plan:** Provide a clear action plan or next steps based on the findings.

In conclusion, effective reporting and presenting of findings are crucial for communicating insights to stakeholders. By following best practices in data visualization, storytelling, and audience tailoring, marketers can create impactful reports and presentations that drive informed decision-making and business success.

and robust analytical tools.

2. Enhanced Insights:

- **Customer Behavior Analysis:** Big data enables more detailed and accurate analysis of customer behavior, preferences, and trends.
- **Predictive Analytics:** By analyzing historical data, predictive models can forecast future behaviors and outcomes, allowing for proactive marketing strategies.
- **Personalization:** Big data supports hyper-personalized marketing efforts by providing deep insights into individual customer preferences and behaviors.

Artificial Intelligence (AI)

AI is transforming marketing analysis by automating complex tasks, providing deeper insights, and enabling more sophisticated strategies.

1. Machine Learning:

- **Pattern Recognition:** Machine learning algorithms can identify patterns and trends in data that are not immediately apparent to human analysts.
- **Predictive Models:** AI-driven predictive models can forecast customer behaviors, market trends, and campaign outcomes with high accuracy.

2. Natural Language Processing (NLP):

- **Sentiment Analysis:** NLP can analyze text data from social media, reviews, and surveys to gauge public sentiment and customer opinions.
- **Chatbots and Virtual Assistants:** AI-powered chatbots enhance customer engagement by providing instant, personalized responses to inquiries.

3. Automation:

- **Automated Reporting:** AI can generate comprehensive reports with minimal human intervention, saving time and reducing the risk of errors.
- **Campaign Optimization:** AI algorithms can automatically adjust marketing campaigns based on real-time performance data, optimizing for better results.

Personalization

Personalization has become a cornerstone of modern marketing, driven by the desire to deliver relevant and meaningful experiences to customers.

1. Dynamic Content:

- **Tailored Messaging:** Personalization tools allow for the creation of dynamic content that adapts to individual user profiles, enhancing relevance and engagement.
- **Product Recommendations:** E-commerce platforms use personalization algorithms to recommend products based on a customer's browsing and purchase history.

2. Customer Journey Mapping:

- **Behavioral Data:** By analyzing behavioral data, marketers can map out individual customer journeys and tailor marketing efforts to each stage.
- **Omni-channel Integration:** Personalization ensures a consistent and seamless experience across all touchpoints, including websites, mobile apps, emails, and in-store interactions.

Trends and Predictions

As technology continues to advance, several emerging trends are set to shape the future of marketing analysis.

1. Increased Use of AI and Automation:

- **AI Integration:** AI will become even more integrated into marketing platforms, providing deeper insights and more automated processes.
- **Voice Search and Assistants:** The rise of voice search and digital assistants will require marketers to optimize for voice-based interactions.

2. Greater Emphasis on Data Privacy:

- **Regulations:** Stricter data privacy regulations (such as GDPR and CCPA) will impact how data is collected, stored, and used. Transparency and compliance will be paramount.
- **Consumer Trust:** Building and maintaining consumer trust through transparent data practices will become increasingly important.

3. Advanced Analytics Techniques:

- **Augmented Analytics:** Combining AI with traditional analytics to enhance human decision-making by providing contextual insights and recommendations.
- **Edge Analytics:** Analyzing data closer to its source (at the edge) to enable faster insights and responses, particularly useful for IoT applications.

4. Enhanced Customer Experiences:

- **Augmented Reality (AR) and Virtual Reality (VR):** These technologies will provide immersive and interactive marketing experiences.
- **Emotional Analytics:** Understanding and responding to customer emotions in real-time to create more engaging and empathetic marketing strategies.

Conclusion

The future of marketing analysis is bright, with numerous advancements poised to enhance how businesses understand and engage with their customers. By staying informed about the latest trends and technologies, marketing analysts can leverage these tools to drive more effective strategies and achieve better results. Embracing big data, AI, and personalization, while remaining mindful of data privacy and evolving consumer expectations, will be crucial for success in this dynamic field.

Glossary & Index

Glossary

Key Terms and Definitions

- **Data Collection**: The process of gathering information from various sources to analyze and make informed decisions.
- **Data Visualization**: The representation of data in graphical format to make complex data more understandable and accessible.
- **Statistical Analysis**: The process of examining data sets to draw conclusions about the information they contain.
- **Market Research**: The action or activity of gathering information about consumers' needs and preferences.
- **Consumer Behavior**: The study of how individuals make decisions to spend their available resources on consumption-related items.
- **SWOT Analysis**: A framework used to evaluate a company's competitive position by identifying its strengths, weaknesses, opportunities, and threats.
- **Key Performance Indicators (KPIs)**: Metrics used to evaluate the success of an organization or a particular activity in which it engages.
- **Competitive Analysis**: The process of identifying and evaluating your competitors' strengths and weaknesses.
- **Benchmarking**: Comparing business processes and performance metrics to industry bests and best practices from other companies.
- **Big Data**: Large and complex data sets that traditional data processing applications are inadequate to handle.
- **Artificial Intelligence (AI)**: The simulation of human intelligence in machines that are programmed to think and learn like humans.
- **Personalization**: Tailoring products, services, or

communications to individual consumers' preferences and behaviors.

Index

A

- Artificial Intelligence (AI), Chapter 10
- Analysis Techniques, Chapter 3, 6

B

- Benchmarking, Chapter 6
- Big Data, Chapter 10

C

- Competitive Analysis, Chapter 6
- Consumer Behavior, Chapter 5

D

- Data Collection, Chapter 3
- Data Visualization, Chapter 2, 9

K

- Key Performance Indicators (KPIs), Chapter 8

M

- Market Research, Chapter 4
- Marketing Strategies, Chapter 7

S